D0975436

Friendship Isn't a Big Thing—It's a Million Little Things

The Art of Female Friendship

Becca Anderson

CORAL GABLES

Published by Mango Publishing Group, a division of Mango Media Inc.

Cover Design: Elina Diaz

Layout Design: Jermaine Lau and Elina Diaz

For permission requests, please contact the publisher at:

Mango Publishing Group
2850 Douglas Road, 2nd Floor
Coral Gables, FL 33134 USA
info@mango.bz

For special orders, quantity sales, course adoptions, and corporate sales, please email the publisher at sales@mango.bz. For trade and wholesale sales, please contact Ingram Publisher Services at customer.service@ingramcontent.com or +1.800.509.4887.

Friendship Isn't a Big Thing—It's a Million Little Things: The Art of Female Friendship

Library of Congress Cataloging
ISBN:(p) 978-1-64250-067-7 (e) 978-1-64250-068-4

Library of Congress Control Number: 2019944130

BISAC category code: FAMILY & RELATIONSHIPS / Friendship

Printed in the United States of America

This book is for my beloved friends Abby, Beth, Leslie, Lillian, Maria, Nancy, and Nina who have been the rudders of my life. You are amazing, incredible, brilliant women, and I will love you forever.

TABLE OF CONTENTS

IN THE COMPANY OF WOMEN

As I write this, I am looking forward to a girlfriends' night out tomorrow evening. Even though we are no longer twentysomethings dancing into the wee hours every weekend, we still get together regularly. Time spent with each other is absolutely essential. Truth be told, it is a combination of group therapy, the latest news, sharing helpful tips and recipes, and a whole lot of what we call processing. We process the state of the world, our jobs, and our relationships. This week, we'll be featuring the "Ex Files." One of my dearest friends has a crazy ex-husband who is a rage texter. And now he has a crazy new girlfriend who completely loses it if any photos of the good old days show up on Facebook or Instagram. Such is life in the twenty-first century where you not only have to plot a course through each day of our over-busy schedules, but also have to navigate the sometimes-tricky waters of social media.

What's a girl to do?

I say we stick with the friends who know us best and see us through all the ups and downs of life; I have always said that our friends are some of the great loves of our lives. My friends have seen me through everything, from crushes and fashion disasters to shared vacations and long, lazy days of sheer delight. They are also there when the chips are down. I have weathered breakups, makeups, financial woes, career crises, and everything in between, thanks to my good friends. Good friends make the world go 'round, so treasure yours, dear reader, and you will reap the benefits tenfold.

In closing, I remind you of the wise words of this memorable wild woman:

*It's the friends you can call up at
4 a.m. that matter.*

—MARLENE DIETRICH

CHAPTER ONE

Sister from Another Mother

I remember my first good friend. I met her in the first week of first grade, and we are still friends today. We could not be more opposite, but, for whatever reason, Abby and I just clicked. We literally saw each other through every stage of life: awkward braces phases, first crushes and first dates, first heartbreaks, homecoming, and prom. I was also a bridesmaid at her wedding. Abby was a child of divorce, and we stayed at each other's houses at least a couple of nights a week. When her father was on dad duty for the weekends, I went trooping along, and went trout fishing and camping with her and her dad, who was a proper Hemingway-esque gentleman. He was also the high school principal and didn't let us get away with a single thing but also instilled a love of literature and nature, as well as stressed the importance of being a life-long learner. Abby's mom was really fun and seemed so glamorous to me. Like Abby, her mom was gorgeous, whip-smart, and gregarious. I can say that I honestly felt like a member of the family and very loved and accepted. Friends are the family we choose, and Abby is truly my sister from another mother.

I bet you have such special sisterly women in your life. Hold on tight and never let them go.

LYLAS! (Love Ya Like A Sister!)

*If you have two friends in your lifetime,
you're lucky. If you have one good friend,
you're more than lucky.*

—S.E. HINTON

She is a friend of my mind. She gather me, man. The pieces I am, she gather them and give them back to me in all the right order.

—TONI MORRISON

Give me one friend, just one, who meets the needs of all my varying moods.

—ESTHER M. CLARK

*There is one friend in the life of each of us
who seems not a separate person, however
dear and beloved, but an expansion,
an interpretation, of one's self, the very
meaning of one's soul.*

—EDITH WHARTON

One friend with whom you have a lot in common is better than three with whom you struggle to find things to talk about. We never needed best friend gear because I guess with real friends you don't have to make it official. It just is.

—MINDY KALING

Your best friend can send your spirits soaring one moment and crush you with a word or gesture the next.

—COLETTE MCBETH

Life is an awful, ugly place to not have a best friend.

—SARAH DESSEN

The biggest ingredient in a best friend is someone whose actions you respect and who you can truly be yourself around.

—RENEE OLSTEAD

*When you meet your best friend in real life,
or you meet your soulmate, you just know
it, and you feel it.*

—LILI REINHART

The idea of losing your best friend,
basically, is the worst thing in world.

—PHOEBE WALLER-BRIDGE

There is nothing I would not do for those who are really my friends.

—JANE AUSTEN

A good relationship has a pattern like a dance and is built on some of the same rules. The partners do not need to hold on tightly, because they move confidently in the same pattern, intricate but gay and swift and free.

—ANNE MORROW LINDBERGH

As we sail through life towards death,
bound unto the same port—heaven,—
Friend, what years could us divide?

—DINAH CRAIK

A friend is someone who reaches for your hand but touches your heart.

—KATHLEEN FROVE

A real friend is one who walks in when the rest of the world walks out.

—JENNIFER ANISTON

When you feel someone else's pain and joy as powerfully as if it were your own, then you know you really loved them.

—ANN BRASHARES

It's not that diamonds are a girl's best friend, but it's your best friends who are your diamonds.

—GINA BARRECA

CHAPTER TWO

Companions through Thick and Thin

Husbands and boyfriends are nice accessories, but girlfriends are the essential must-haves of life. It's our gal pals who get us through both good times and bad. The course of my life has been charted over coffee with the girls, new plans made over a margarita (or two), and many a late-night phone call dedicated to the topic of love. Who else do we turn to for the best advice, gossip, and fashion tips? There are many different aspects of friendship—from sharing secrets to sharing tears, and from being each other's cheerleaders to comforting one another with hugs and good advice. I once had such a bad breakup that my friend Leslie came over, scooped me up, and installed me in her spare bedroom, where I curled up into a fetal position for days. I was in such bad shape that I couldn't even speak, but she was there for me and surrounded me with a secure blanket of unconditional love and understanding. No judgment; just support. After a few days, I crawled out of my cocoon. Not exactly a butterfly, but I was wiser, and I learned something far more important than any lesson about the travails of romance. I learned that the bonds of true friendship are stronger than anything. For better or worse, your friends are there for you when you need them.

Walking with a friend in the dark is better than walking alone in the light.

—HELEN KELLER

Time spent with friends is healing because we don't perceive it as time. We just are.

—GRACE MORTON

Trouble is like a sieve through which we sift our acquaintances. Those too big to pass through are our friends.

—ARLENE FRANCIS

*Life's truest happiness is found in friendships
we make along the way.*

—LAUREN RUIZ

Loneliness is the most terrible poverty.

—MOTHER TERESA

Some people go to priests; others to poetry; I to my friends.

—VIRGINIA WOOLF

A friend is one who overlooks your broken fence and admires the flowers in your garden.

—UNKNOWN

The friend who holds your hand and says the wrong thing is made of dearer stuff than the one who stays away.

—BARBARA KINGSOLVER

Parents start you off on life, but friends get you through it.

—D E E   C H O U

A friend is someone who knows the song in your heart and can sing it back to you when you have forgotten the words.

—DONNA ROBERTS

I am treating you as my friend, asking you to share my present minuses in the hope I can ask you to share my future pluses.

—KATHERINE MANSFIELD

I don't know what I would have done so many times in my life if I hadn't had my girlfriends.

—REESE WITHERSPOON

If you can find a group of women, any age, who are supportive and kind and love you, that's the best. I have a group of girlfriends that I would lie in front of a bus for. They've picked me up through really, really bad times, and I can definitely say I've done the same for them.

—KATIE LOWES

Lots of people want to ride with you in the limo, but what you want is someone who will take the bus with you when the limo breaks down.

—OPRAH WINFREY

Sweat makes good friendship cement.

—TYNE DALY

It is better to be in chains with friends than in a garden with strangers.

—PERSIAN PROVERB

Friends are the thermometers by which we may judge the temperature of our fortunes.

—COUNTESS OF BLESSINGTON

We have been friends together

In sunshine and in shade.

—CAROLINE E. S. NORTON

If you can survive eleven days in cramped quarters with a friend and come out laughing, your friendship is the real deal.

—OPRAH WINFREY

I don't mind whether a person is rich or poor. Once my friend, always my friend.

—TSARINA ALEXANDRA

Women are like tea bags. You never know how strong they are until you put them in hot water.

—ELEANOR ROOSEVELT

CHAPTER THREE
Laughing It Up

I don't know about you, but I can lose my sense of humor at times. I get stressed out and my funny bone just disappears. Ladies, this is when we need our friends the most. As the old saying goes, laughter truly is the best medicine, and giggling with your gal pals can heal almost anything. My friend Leslie has an irrepressible sense of humor, and she cracks me up right when I need it. Her mother's health is failing, her husband got laid off, and she has two kids in college, but she can still whip up a fabulous dinner for us and we talk about everything. Leslie's genius is that she knows worrying about things never helps anything and actually makes it worse. What does help? Getting really silly! We talk about old times and memories of crazy outfits we thought were the height of fashion. Thinking back to the early days of our friendship is sheer delight. This year, she inspired me to do a Christmas tree decorated with my crazy earrings from back in the day. It actually looks pretty good but is also so ridiculous that people can't help but laugh at it. A lot.

For years, my signature look was to wear the biggest, blingiest earrings I could get my hands on one. Who knew they would make the best holiday ornaments? Leslie did! And now, we will get many more years of fun out of my crazy fashion don'ts. Listen up ladies, laugh it up with your friends every chance you get!

A friend is someone who knows all about you and loves you anyway!

—NANCY LAUREN FISH

The friends with whom I sat on graduation day have been my friends for life. They are my children's godparents, the people to whom I've been able to turn in times of trouble, friends who have been kind enough not to sue me when I've used their names for Death Eaters.

—J.K. ROWLING

It seems to me that trying to live without friends is like milking a bear to get cream for your morning coffee. It is a whole lot of trouble and then not worth much after you get it.

—ZORA NEALE HURSTON

Count your joys instead of your woes;
count your friends instead of your foes.

—IRISH PROVERB

If I killed somebody, I have zero doubt that if I called my best friend and was like, "Hey, grab a shovel," she wouldn't even ask the question.

—MILA KUNIS

Four be the things I am wiser to know:
Idleness, sorrow, a friend, and a foe.

—DOROTHY PARKER

A good friend brings out the best in everybody!

—MIMI COOKE

I have lost friends, some by death [...] others through sheer inability to cross the street.

—VIRGINIA WOOLF

No one will ever be as entertained by us as us.

—U N K N O W N

There is nothing better than a friend, unless
it is a friend with chocolate.

—LINDA GRAYSON

*There are very few honest friends—the
demand is not particularly great.*

—MARIE VON EBNER-ESCHENBACH

I do not want people to be very agreeable, as it saves me the trouble of liking them a great deal.

—JANE AUSTEN

If you seek friends who can be trusted, go to the cemetery.

—RUSSIAN PROVERB

*There is nothing like puking with somebody
to make you into old friends.*

—SYLVIA PLATH

I have a lot of good friends and not one of them has ever introduced themselves by saying, "I'm a very good friend."

—CHELSEA HANDLER

True friends don't judge each other, they judge other people together.

— EMILIE SAINT-GENIS

The best time to make friends is before you need them.

—ETHEL BARRYMORE

In the cookie of life, friends are the chocolate chips.

—UNKNOWN

*I've always believed that a goal in
life is not to own a boat but to have a friend
with a boat.*

—CHRISTIE HEFNER

CHAPTER FOUR

Tips for True Friends

While I have spent a lot of hours with friends, laughing, crying, and watching movies, I'm not an expert on keeping friendships green and growing. In my younger, more insecure days, I was often unsure whether my friends actually enjoyed spending time with me, or if I was simply someone who was invited because I was an acknowledged part of the group. I spent hours finding and baking new desserts for each gathering, trying to bribe my way into their affections, rather than just spending time and talking to them, which meant it took longer for them to get to know me, and I them!

My amateur advice? Just relax and be yourself. Your true friends will enjoy spending time with you no matter what, but they will always appreciate some peanut butter fudge too.

If you judge people, you have no time to love them.

—MOTHER TERESA

Plant a seed of friendship—reap a bouquet of happiness.

—LOIS L. KAUFMAN

*There may not be a recipe for friendship,
but that doesn't mean there are no rules.*

—BLANCHE HARDING

*The only thing to do is to hug one's friends
tight and do one's job.*

—EDITH WHARTON

Abandon the cultural myth that all female friendships must be bitchy, toxic, or competitive. This myth is like heels and purses—pretty but designed to SLOW women down.

—ROXANE GAY

I don't get women who pick fights with their friends. It's not like you get to kiss and make up afterwards. Play those games with your lover if you have to, but don't toy with a good friendship.

—MARCIA BOND

You can hardly make a friend in a year, but you can easily lose one in an hour.

—CHINESE PROVERB

As hard as it is and as tired as I am, I force myself to get dinner at least once a week with my girlfriends or have a sleepover. Otherwise my life is just work.

—JENNIFER LAWRENCE

Remember, "No one's more important than people!" In other words, friendship is the most important thing not career or housework, or one's fatigue and it needs to be tended and nurtured.

—JULIA CHILD

Send a thank-you note to a good friend, a relative, or coworker "just because" and let them know what you appreciate about them. This "attitude of gratitude" will take you far in your life and will come back to you many times over.

—MARY JANE RYAN

Do not save your loving speeches for your friends till they are dead; do not write them on their tombstones, speak them rather now instead.

—ANNA CUMMINS

Keep what is worth keeping and with the breath of kindness blow the rest away.

—DINAH CRAIK

Live with intention. Walk to the edge. Listen Hard. Practice wellness. Play with abandon. Laugh. Choose with no regret. Appreciate your friends. Continue to learn. Do what you love. Live as if this is all there is.

—MARY ANNE RADMACHER

Our instinct is to think about the bad things happening in our lives, but at the end of the day it's always more about the people who love you.

— ZENDAYA

Friendship with oneself is all-important, because without it, one cannot be friends with anybody else in the world.

—ELEANOR ROOSEVELT

It is worse to mistrust a friend than to be deceived by him.

—FRENCH PROVERB

True friends are like diamonds—bright, beautiful, valuable, and always in style.

—NICOLE RICHIE

Though friendship is not quick to burn, it is explosive stuff.

—MAY SARTON

*The character of a man depends on
whether he has good or bad friends.*

—JAPANESE PROVERB

Friendship isn't a big thing—it's a million little things.

—ANONYMOUS

If friends disappoint you over and over,
that's in large part your own fault.
Once someone has shown a tendency to
be self-centered, you need to recognize
that and take care of yourself; people
aren't going to change simply because you
want them to.

—OPRAH WINFREY

CHAPTER FIVE

Faraway Friends

Here is my favorite thing about long-distance besties; it can be years since you have seen each other and, the minute you start talking, it is like you were never apart. That is a sign of a true bond and the strength of that connection, no matter how many miles are between you. Of course, you would rather live in the same 'hood or a quick drive away, but modern living can mean a lot of travel for work, bicoastal lifestyles, fantastic job opportunities a continent away, or any number of reasons why you go from weekly hang time to finding yourselves in different time zones. Nevertheless, you'll persist.

My dearly beloved Maria moved to Hotlanta when her groom got an amazing execute position at a major corporation with the requisite complicated, fancy title. We were bereft, but it was such a marvelous opportunity, they had to take it. After much wringing of hands and more goodbyes than the extended director's cut of *The Fellowship of the Ring*, they U-Hauled three thousand miles to their new destiny. Yet we haven't missed a beat. We keep up as though she was down the block.

No matter how many miles, a good friendship makes any distance nonexistent. Good friends are worth hanging onto and make reunions all the sweeter!

A friendship can weather most things and thrive in thin soil; but it needs a little mulch of letters and phone calls and small, silly presents every so often—just to save it from drying out completely.

—PAM BROWN

There is magic in long-distance friendships. They let you relate to other human beings in a way that goes beyond being physically together and is often more profound.

—DIANA CORTES

There is no distance too great between friends, for love gives wings to the heart.

—ELIZABETH E. KOEHLER

Though our communication wanes at times of absence, I'm aware of a strength that emanates in the background.

—CLAUDETTE RENNER

There is a natural ebb and flow to friendships. There are times you think there's nothing left between you, that you've hit the bottom, but the special ones survive, find ways of restoring themselves.

—COLETTE MCBETH

*In loneliness, in sickness, in confusion—
the mere knowledge of friendship makes
it possible to endure, even if the friend
is powerless to help. It is enough that
they exist.*

—PAM BROWN

How we need another soul to cling to.

—SYLVIA PLATH

The most beautiful discovery that true friends can make is that you can grow separately without growing apart.

—ELIZABETH FOLEY

True friends are never apart, maybe in distance but never in heart.

—UNKNOWN

True friendship resists time, distance, and silence.

—ISABEL ALLENDE

*I know I've got the right friends because
they understand when they haven't seen
me for three months and then when I do see
them, it's exactly as it was before.*

—JESSIE J

True friends are always together in spirit.

—L.M. MONTGOMERY

I still have friends from primary school. And my two best girlfriends are from secondary school. I don't have to explain anything to them. I don't have to apologize for anything. They know. There's no judgment in any way.

—EMMA WATSON

Growing apart doesn't change the fact that for a long time we grew side by side; our roots will always be tangled. I'm glad for that.

—ALLY CONDIE

Good friends are like stars. You don't always see them, but you know they're always there.

—U N K N O W N

CHAPTER SIX

Girlfriends, new and old

You never know when life will gift you a new friend. One sure way to know is that you immediately feel comfortable with them. Somehow, they are just an easy fit in your life. My pal Nancy is an example of that. She was the partner of one of my best guy friends, and, after they split, I didn't see her for some years. I had always liked her during brief encounters from before and was sad when things didn't work out between her and Roger. However, I ran into her at a writers' conference, and she seemed happy and upbeat and had returned to college once her son graduated from high school. I thought that was a bold, brave move. We met for tea, and it turned out we have SO MUCH in common! She is an adventurous spirit and likes to try things and inspired me to do the same. We are fellow explorers and I so admire her commitment to being a lifelong learner. Roger seemed nonplused at first, but now he is happy about this new friendship that was born from an old one. Be on the lookout for your new companions (while always making time for the old); they could be right around the corner!

Each friend represents a world in us, a world possibly not born until they arrive, and it is only by this meeting that a new world is born.

—ANAÏS NIN

A friend is like a four-leaf clover, hard to find but lucky to have.

—SAMANTHA ROSALES

A new friendship is like an unripened fruit—it may become either an orange or a lemon.

—EMMA STACEY

They call it "making friends" for a reason.
It takes effort, and the right ingredients.

—SANDRA GARRETT

It takes a lot of courage to show your dreams to someone else.

—ERMA BOMBECK

Make new friends and keep the old; one is silver and the other's gold.

—GIRL SCOUT MOTTO

*Strangers are just friends waiting
to happen!*

—WENDY WENTWORTH

Ah, how good it feels...the hand of an old friend.

—MARY ENGELBREIT

The companions of our childhood always possess a certain power over our minds which hardly any later friend can obtain.

—MARY SHELLEY

We are friends for life. When we're together the years fall away. Isn't that what matters? To have someone who can remember with you? To have someone who remembers how far you've come?

—JUDY BLUME

Yes'm, old friends is always best, 'less you can catch a new one that's fit to make an old one out of.

—SARAH ORNE JEWETT

Friendship starts out free and becomes priceless with time.

—ELLIE SHOJA

Constant use will not wear ragged the fabric of friendship.

—D O R O T H Y   P A R K E R

I don't know about you, but my girlfriends have been my girlfriends forever, and they're my sisters and my family.

—ELIZABETH OLSEN

Some people need a red carpet rolled out in front of them in order to walk forward into friendship. They can't see the tiny outstretched hands all around them, everywhere, like leaves on trees.

—MIRANDA JULY

Some people arrive and make such a beautiful impact on your life, you can barely remember what life was like without them.

—ANNA TAYLOR

Friendship however is a plant which cannot be forced—true friendship is no gourd springing up in a night and withering in a day.

—CHARLOTTE BRONTË

We will need to become savvy about how to build relationships, how to nurture growing, evolving things.

—MARGARET WHEATLEY

Nobody sees a flower really; it is so small.
We haven't time, and to see takes time—
like to have a friend takes time.

—GEORGIA O'KEEFFE

CHAPTER SEVEN

Girl Talk (Except When No Words Are Needed)

You can tell when women have been friends for a long time. If you observe them even for a short time, you'll see they have their own language. Some of this language does not even involve words! There will be various vocalizations, ranging from murmurs to grunts to guffaws, that say a whole lot without saying a word. The more enduring the duo, the more evolved the secret language is. It must also be said that a lot of communication also involves no sound; ever notice how your girlfriend can point with her head to a rack of clothes, and you know exactly which sweater she wanted you to try on? Or when you're out on the town and she gently nudges you with the toe of her shoe in just such a way that you know she wants you to know you are being checked out by the cute guy by the bar but you must not look up quite yet. Here's what I know for sure about girl talk. It can be anything and on any topic. Just keep communicating with each other, and the world will be a better place for it.

For women, talk is the glue that holds relationships together; it creates connections between people and a sense of community.

—DEBORAH FARMER

The sharing of joy, whether physical, emotional, psychic, or intellectual, forms a bridge between the sharers which can be the basis for understanding much of what is not shared between them, and lessens the threat of their difference.

—AUDRE LORDE

A good friend is cheaper than therapy.

—U N K N O W N

Silences make the real conversations between friends. Not the saying but the never needing to say is what counts.

—MARGARET LEE RUNBECK

"Stay" is a charming word in a friend's vocabulary.

—LOUISA MAY ALCOTT

You never lose by loving. You always lose by holding back.

—BARBARA DE ANGELIS

We all need friends with whom we can speak of our deepest concerns, and who do not fear to speak the truth in love to us.

—REV. MARGARET GUENTHER

All you'll get from strangers is surface pleasantry or indifference. Only someone who loves you will criticize you.

—JUDITH CRIST

It's important for our friends to believe that we are unreservedly frank with them, and important to the friendship that we are not.

—MIGNON MCLAUGHLIN

No person is your friend who demands your silence or denies your right to grow.

—ALICE WALKER

The blessing it is to have a friend to whom one can speak fearlessly on any subject; with whom one's deepest as well as one's most foolish thoughts come out simply and safely.

—DINAH CRAIK

Talk between women friends is always therapy...

—JAYNE ANNE PHILLIPS

I possess the faculty of enjoying the company of...my friends as well in silence as in conversation.

—ANNE BRONTË

Women understand. We may share experiences, make jokes, paint pictures, and describe humiliations that mean nothing to men, but women understand.

—GLORIA STEINEM

The finest kind of friendship is between two people who expect a great deal of each other, but never ask it.

—SYLVIA BREMER

The only people you can really share certain things with in secret are your girlfriends.

—SHIRLEY KNIGHT

Honesty is the quality I value most in a friend. Not bluntness, but honesty with compassion.

—BROOKE SHIELDS

I think a good friend, to me, is all about trust and loyalty. You don't ever want to second-guess whether you can tell your friend something.

—LAUREN CONRAD

Friends are those rare people who ask how you are and then wait for the answer.

—UNKNOWN

CHAPTER EIGHT

With a Little Help from My Friends

When I really stop to consider, many of the best things in my life have happened because of the kindness of not strangers, but friends. I got into book publishing because my friend Maria had the deep insight that was the right career for me. I had gotten a promotion in import-export and was set to travel the world as a buyer for an international corporation, only to learn that children were making the products in China and India. When my boss showed me photos of the factories we were going to visit, I asked him about the children. He flatly stated they were very happy to have jobs, adding, "You should be too." In that moment, I knew I had to quit and did immediately. The look on his face was sheer astonishment. I packed up my few things, grabbed my purse and keys, and drove back across the Bay Bridge to my tiny apartment in San Francisco, wondering how I was going pay rent on the first of the next month. I ran inside, flung myself on the bed, and called Maria. She listened intently and said, "Your favorite thing is reading and talking about books. Maybe you should be in publishing." Maria knew I was in bad shape both financially and emotionally, so she offered to help me with the job search. She also told me I had done the right thing in quitting that job, and I needed to hear that. As it turned about, Maria was exactly right in her career advice. I am proud to add that I was part of a task force that rated printers in other countries to make sure no children were involved in the manufacture of books. All with a little help from my friends.

If you want to go fast, go alone. If you want to go far, go together.

—AFRICAN PROVERB

A friend is someone who makes it easy to believe in yourself.

—HEIDI WILLS

Friends are like angels following you through life.

—MARY ELLEN

My friends are my estate.

—EMILY DICKINSON

*Never doubt that a small group of
dedicated people can make a difference.
Indeed, it is the only thing that ever has.*

—MARGARET MEAD

I've always believed that one woman's success can only help another woman's success.

—GLORIA VANDERBILT

We are each other's magnitude and bond.

—GWENDOLYN BROOKS

Women hold up half the sky.

—CHINESE PROVERB

Other people and other people's ideas are often better than your own. Find a group of people who challenge and inspire you, spend a lot of time with them, and it will change your life.

—AMY POEHLER

I can trust my friends. These people force me to examine, encourage me to grow.

—CHER

A friend will stand for you when you are no longer able. A woman can say to herself, "If I die, I know that my friend, my sister-friend will be here to hold up the banner."

—MAYA ANGELOU

Female friendship has been the bedrock of women's lives for as long as there have been women.

—REBECCA TRAISTER

Female friendships that work are relationships in which women help each other belong to themselves.

—LOUISE BERNIKOW

Behind every successful woman is a tribe of other successful women who have her back.

—ANONYMOUS

Female friendships are important because they help define us in a particular time and place.

—VICTORIA SCOTT

To be rich in friends is to be poor in nothing.

—LILIAN WHITING

Anything is possible when you have the right people there to support you.

—MISTY COPELAND

I thank you, God in Heaven, for friends.

—MARGARET ELIZABETH SANGSTER

Friends and good manners will carry you where money won't go.

—MARGARET WALKER

CHAPTER NINE

Friends Are Some of the Great Loves of Our Lives

Here is the straight truth: you will experience breakups, and the odds are 50/50 that you will get a divorce. Some of us, myself included, will also grieve a partner. That shock came like a bolt out of the blue, and diagnosis to death was less than a year. Not only do you barely have time to accept the prognosis and try to deal with it in a supportive way, but when a life is cut short at such a young age, it is nearly impossible to be able to process it. As they say, "life comes at you fast," and death comes even faster. Along with it comes a lot of paperwork and the business side that won't wait for anyone. It is very difficult to sort through a loved one's things when you can barely function, and every single thing is a memory. I can tell you that I would not even be here if it were not for my friends. They gathered around me and helped take care of memorials, organizing, bills, and even simple things like buying groceries and taking out the trash when I was in the fetal position. Needless to say, that remains one of the hardest times I ever went through, but, a couple of years down the road, I was able to realize that my friends are my Soul Tribe and they enfolded me with so much love that they essentially brought me back to life when I was so sad, I was not sure I could carry on. Friends are some of the greatest loves of our lives. Everything you give to your dearest friends, you will receive back a thousandfold.

The best way to mend a broken heart is time and girlfriends.

—GWYNETH PALTROW

I feel there's so much pressure, especially for women, to declare what their life's going to be and what their career is, and "Are you married yet? Are you single? But you're thirty." And girlfriends are so important. You can have a boyfriend or husband when you're thirty, but you still need your girlfriends.

—KRISTEN WIIG

Well, it seems to me that the best relationships—the ones that last—are frequently the ones that are rooted in friendship.

—GILLIAN ANDERSON

Friendship is certainly the finest balm for the pangs of disappointed love.

—JANE AUSTEN

It's important to have girlfriends, because guys tend to come and go.

—ASHLEY TISDALE

Well, female friendships are extraordinary. They don't have to be sexual to be intense love affairs. A breakup with a female friend can be more traumatic than a breakup with a lover.

—KEIRA KNIGHTLEY

My true friends have always given me that supreme proof of devotion, a spontaneous aversion to the man I loved.

—COLETTE

Female friendship was one-tenth prevention and nine-tenths cleanup.

—MAGGIE SHIPSTEAD

Whether you're throwing up or breaking up, you want your girlfriend right there!

—DREW BARRYMORE

It's bullshit to think of friendship and romance as being different. They're not. They're just variations of the same love. Variations of the same desire to be close.

—RACHEL COHN

Sometimes being a friend means mastering the art of timing. There is a time for silence. A time to let go and allow people to hurl themselves into their own destiny. And a time to prepare to pick up the pieces when it's all over.

—OCTAVIA E. BUTLER

You're always in love with your best friend.
That's why you're best friends.

—KATIE STEVENS

Men come and go—God knows they certainly have in my life—but girlfriends are forever. I have a lot of girlfriends but only a few very, very close ones.

—ALANA STEWART

I love my husband, but it is nothing like a conversation with a woman that understands you. I grow so much from those conversations.

—BEYONCÉ

Everybody understands friendship, and friendship is different than love—it's a different kind of love. Friendship has more freedom, more latitude. You don't expect your friend to be as you think your friend should be; you expect your friend just to love you as a friend.

—CAROLE KING

We need to stick together and see there's more to life than pleasing men. It's important not to cut yourself off from female friendships. I think sometimes girls get scared of other girls, but you need each other.

—ZOOEY DESCHANEL

Friendships between women, as any woman will tell you, are built of a thousand small kindnesses...swapped back and forth and over again.

—MICHELLE OBAMA

*Of all the pleasures of marriage, friendship
has got to be one of the best.*

—FAWN WEAVER

CHAPTER TEN

Time Well Spent Together

Celebrate your friends. Don't wait for birthdays; ordinary days become extraordinary in the company of your besties. Friendships are just like any other relationship, and they need to be nurtured and tended. Go out for coffee, brunch, drinks—have your friends over for a movie night pajama party sleepover, go camping, take trips, get lost together, and share adventures. Whatever you do, just spend as much time together as you can. The memories you make will become bonds of friendship that strengthen over time. It really doesn't matter what you do, just so long as you do it together. And always remember that friendship is not a big thing, it is a million little things.

It's my women friends that keep starch in my spine, and without them, I don't know where I would be. We have to just hang together and help each other.

—JANE FONDA

Once a month, I get together with my girlfriends, and we usually check into a hotel or go to someone else's house. We can talk for fifteen hours, and it just flies by.

—LESLIE MANN

Friends are thieves of time.

—LATIN PROVERB

Sometimes, walking with a friend,
I forget the world.

—GRACE PALEY

You know when I feel inwardly beautiful? When I am with my girlfriends and we are having a goddess circle.

—JENNIFER ANISTON

*We cherish our friends not for their ability
to amuse us, but for ours to amuse them.*

—EVELYN WAUGH

I think that it's really important to have good friends. Nowadays, you can text twenty-four hours a day and be in constant contact, but, every once in a while, it's nice to just get out with your girlfriends and have fun.

—AMANDA SCHULL

*What's really important in life—friends,
friends, friends.*

—FANNIE FLAGG

*Happiness is the comfortable
companionship of friends.*

—PAM BROWN

My idea of good company is the company of clever, well-informed people who have a great deal of conversation.

—JANE AUSTEN

No one can be happy in eternal solitude.

—ANNE BRONTË

There is no happiness like that of being loved by your fellow creatures, and feeling that your presence is an addition to their comfort.

—CHARLOTTE BRONTË

My girlfriends are everything to me. They celebrate with you, they cry with you, they hold you when you need to be held. They laugh with you. They're mean with you! They're always there, and it's just a priceless thing to have.

—JENNIFER LOPEZ

Women instinctually know how to nourish each other, and just being with each other is restorative.

—TANJA TAALJARD

A Girl's Night In to Remember

My besties and I like to have a cup of tea now and again, occasionally the fancy kind with teacakes, cupcakes, and cookies that are almost too beautiful to eat. During my decade in the Lower Haight, my dear friends got together once a month, taking turns at each other's houses. I was excited to be hosting one lovely, late spring day and planned everything to a tee—lemon bars with lime icing, mini-cupcakes with icing that looked like lace, and my favorite black and white cookies: chocolate on one side and vanilla on the other. I even had brightly colored paper napkins with sassy wild women quotes on them.

I was working in Berkeley and living in San Francisco, which meant that just getting across the Bay Bridge was an adventure. On this day, it was going to be a miracle. I was terrified my friends would be standing at the front door, stamping their nicely shod feet and waiting for me as I navigated traffic.

I surrendered to it, knowing my anxiety would not change a thing. Plus, I had my secret weapon—the nicest array of confections ever. How could they be mad at me when they were being served stunningly beautiful cookies on napkins that reminded them they are fabulous?

Finally, my lane of traffic oozed off the Fremont exit into Downtown San Francisco. I planned to bust one of my special moves and drive down a one-way arterial to avoid the clogged streets. To do that, I had to drive past the TransBay Terminal, one of the most desolate and derelict spots in all of the greater Bay Area. I was chugging along and feeling good about my bag of goodies, when I was stopped again by a Muni bus that appeared to be lumbering along at maybe three miles per hour. But I still had my special treats, and my confidence remained intact. I looked to my left, and a mother and her toddler were standing on the raised median, not two feet away from my car. She looked to be not much older than a teenager herself and had a big bruise on her cheek and a frightened look. Her little boy was hugging her knee, trying to stay warm in the arctic wind that blasts downtown SF as soon as the sun sets. I smiled at them, and she smiled back; I saw she was missing at least one tooth. In that moment, I just knew she had run away from an abusive home and was getting herself and her son to safety. I also knew that they needed money and I scrabbled around in my messy purse but could only find a five-dollar bill, as I had spent all my cash on the sweets. I grabbed the pretty paper bag filled with boxes of delicacies and shoved it into her hands, along with the wadded-up five-dollar bill. The look on her face was what will stay with me a lifetime; she was surprised, the stress drained out of her face, and I could see how pretty she was. The bus shot foreword, and, as I started driving away, I managed to shout back at her, "These are the best cookies in the world, so everything is going to be ok!" I looked in the rearview mirror and saw her bend down, open a box, and lovingly feed her little boy one of my treasured black and whites. They were laughing, and her son was even kind of dancing around. My heart lifted as I drove away. I was especially pleased that this young woman was going to be reminded about her fabulousness by sassy paper napkins.

My girlfriends and I ate microwaved popcorn that night, but nobody minded. We also ended up having a much deeper and richer discussion about real things, no shop or shopping talk, no boyfriend problems. We talked about how lucky we were and ways we could give back to the world.

It is funny how I knew those cookies were going to save the night. I guess I just didn't know whose.

About the Author

Becca Anderson comes from a long line of teachers and preachers from Ohio and Kentucky. The teacher side of her family led her to become a woman's studies scholar and the author of the bestselling *The Book of Awesome Women*. An avid collector of affirmations, meditations, prayers, and blessings, she helps run a "Gratitude and Grace Circle" that meets monthly at homes, churches, and bookstores in the San Francisco Bay Area where she currently resides. Becca Anderson credits her spiritual practice and daily prayers with helping her recover from a major health challenge and wants to share this encouragement with anyone who is facing difficulty in life with *Prayers for Hard Times* and *The Woman's Book of Prayer*.

The author of *Badass Affirmations* and *Every Day Thankful*, Becca Anderson shares prayers, affirmations, inspirational writings, and suggested acts of kindness at thedailyinspoblog.wordpress.com.

She also blogs about Awesome Women at theblogofawesomewomen.wordpress.com.

@AndersonBecca_ on Twitter
@BeccaAndersonWriter on Facebook
@BeccaAndersonWriter on Instagram

Also by

Becca Anderson

Every Day Thankful

The Book of Awesome Women

Prayers for Hard Times

Badass Women Give the Best Advice

Badass Affirmations

The Woman's Book of Prayer

The Crafty Gardener

The Buddha's Guide to Gratitude